MONTANA
for Kids

Allen Morris Jones

Published in the United States by

Bangtail Press
P.O. Box 11262
Bozeman, MT 59719

www.bangtailpress.com

Cover Images: wolf silhouette, lilac / shutterstock.com; geese, VladimirCeresnak / shutterstock.com

For Corey

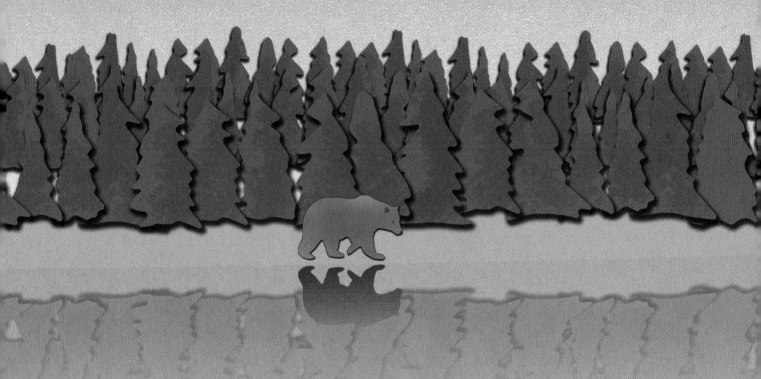

This is Montana

It's a pretty awesome state. It's kind of a rectangle, but with a cool little squiggly line along the western edge.

We have a bunch of mountain ranges, mostly in the west, and open plains, mostly in the east. We have three major river systems and two national parks. We also have a Continental Divide, which means that the water in the western part of the state flows west and the water in the eastern part flows east.

If you're reading this, it's probably because you either live here or are visiting or are planning a visit. Or maybe you're just curious.

In any case, I'm betting that we're on the same page, awesome-state wise.

Montana: Pre-You

If you already know a bit about Montana, you know that there are all sorts of things to see and do here. You can ski and hike, hunt and fish, camp and float. Or you can just take a drive with the grown-ups.

People who live in Montana have all sorts of different jobs. They're ranchers and farmers, doctors and nurses, engineers and teachers. When they're not working, chances are

they like to ski or hike or fish or camp or float.

It's all pretty cool. But the thing is, you can't *really* understand what a place is all about until you know what happened before you arrived.

That's what history really is. It's the story of a place before you came onto the scene.

And that's what this book is for: to tell you just a little bit about Montana, pre-you.

First Peoples

The story of Montana begins with the first peoples. For thousands of years before the rest of the world even knew a place like Montana existed, the area was inhabited by tribes of native peoples. Some of the tribes in Eastern Montana had names like the Cheyenne, Crow, Blackfeet, Assiniboine, Gros Ventre, Cree, and Chippewa. Other tribes with names like the Shoshone, Kootenai, Salish, and Pend d'Oreille lived in Western Montana.

Each tribe had its own language, belief system, and tribal leaders. The tribes had their own names for themselves, too. The Crow called themselves the Apsáalooke, for instance, while the Blackfeet called themselves the Niitsitapi.

When immigrants arrived, they also brought new diseases with them. Between conflicts with the newcomers and disease, some of the tribes nearly disappeared. Some *did* disappear. It's one of the saddest stories you'll ever read.

Today, the languages and traditions of the remaining tribes continue on, kept alive by the heroes of their people.

"At the Water's Edge, Piegan,"
by Edward S. Curtis

Horses

When most people hear the word Montana, they might think of the Old West, of cowboys and Indians and horses. But horses weren't always here. Horses came to America in the 1500s with the first Spanish explorers.

Trading and raiding between tribes gradually brought horses to Montana. Most tribes in the area had horses by the mid to late 1700s.

Horses changed everything for the first peoples. Before horses, Indians used dogs to help them carry their belongings. They would stack their items on a pole frame called a travois (truh-voy), and then a dog would pull the travois.

After horses arrived, the Indians could travel further and faster. They could also more easily hunt buffalo and other large animals.

Some tribes, like the Crow, became famous for their skill with horses.

"Nez Perce Warrior," by Edward S. Curtis

Bison

For Plains Indians, few animals were as important as bison, also called buffalo. In Montana, some tribes hunted bison from horseback with bows and arrows, and later with rifles. They also drove herds of them off of certain cliffs, called buffalo jumps.

When historians talk about bison, they can't help but mention all the ways the animals could be used. If you were Indian, you ate the meat, but you also used the skins for clothing and tepees. The bones could be made into knives and scrapers and clubs, and the hooves could be boiled into glue.

The horns became cups and spoons. For some tribes, a buffalo hunt must have been a little bit like a trip to the grocery store for us.

In the early 1800s, there were as many as 50 million buffalo in the West. But by the late 1800s, they were almost all gone. Small herds lived on in Yellowstone National Park and a few other places, including some Indian reservations in Montana. All of the thousands of bison living today are descended from these small herds.

Lewis and Clark

In 1804, President Thomas Jefferson sent Meriwether Lewis, William Clark, and a group of other brave men on an expedition. The group was called the Corps of Discovery. Their job was to explore the country from west of the Mississippi River to the Pacific Ocean. The United States had just bought a huge portion of this territory from France, and very few Easterners had been there.

The trip took two-and-a-half years. At one point, the Corps had to carry their boats around the great falls of the Missouri. A Shoshone woman named Sakajawea served as a guide, and later helped them trade for horses.

The Corps spent their second winter beside the Pacific Ocean. On the way home, Lewis and Clark went back through what would become Montana.

"Lewis and Clark at Three Forks," by Edgar S. Paxson

Lewis went north on the Missouri River while Clark went south along the Yellowstone River. Clark named a big rock formation on the Yellowstone after Sakajawea's baby. He called it "Pompey's Pillar."

Lewis and Clark covered more than 8,000 miles on their trip. They mostly walked or traveled in boats but sometimes they rode horses, too. The journals that Lewis and Clark wrote on their journey became very famous.

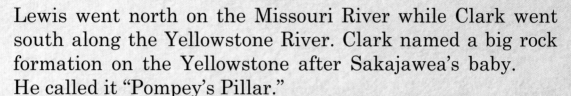

The route taken by the Corps of Discovery.

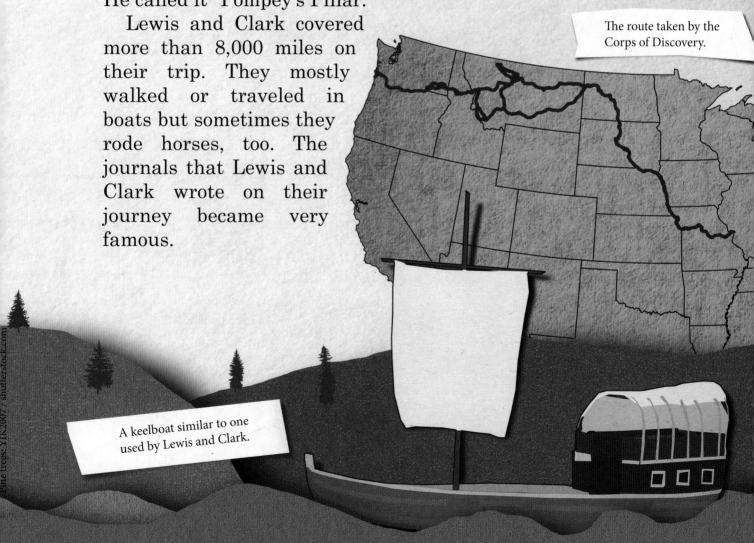

A keelboat similar to one used by Lewis and Clark.

Mountain Men

On their way home, Lewis and Clark met several groups of fur trappers traveling back up the Missouri River. These trappers, and others like them, are what we now call mountain men.

Most mountain men worked for one of a few different fur companies. They traveled all around the West, trapping beavers for their skins. Fashionable people in the East liked to wear hats that were made out of beaver skins.

The work to trap these beaver was quite hard. Think about standing all day long in ice-cold water, setting heavy iron traps. Plus, Indian tribes often didn't like it that trappers were in the area without their permission. It could be dangerous work, too.

"Mountain Man,"
by Alfred Jacob Miller

Once a year, mountain men would get together for a big party they called a rendezvous (rond-ay-vu). This was when they sold the beaver pelts they'd been collecting. They also bought everything they might need to live and work in the wilderness for another year.

When beaver skin hats went out of fashion, and when the beaver became scarce, mountain men found other ways to make their livings. Some even began to work as guides, helping others travel into Montana.

John Colter

One of the first mountain men was named John Colter. He traveled with Lewis and Clark, and later was the first Easterner to see what would become Yellowstone Park. He told wild stories about bubbling mud-pots and shooting geysers. He was also known for escaping the Blackfeet near what's now Three Forks, Montana.

Colter and a friend were trapping beaver in the area, even though they knew the Indians probably wouldn't like it. When they were captured, Colter's friend was killed. Colter was given a second chance, though. The Indians took his shoes and clothes, then told him to start running.

He ran for a long way, outracing a crowd of warriors. He killed the fastest one, then hid in a beaver dam until the Blackfeet left. But now he was left naked and alone in the middle of Montana. A week later, he walked into a fort on the Big Horn River, very hungry but still alive.

Miners

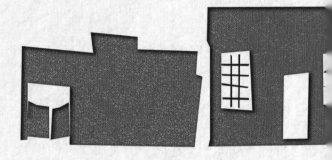

While people have come to Montana for many reasons, one of the most common reasons has been to strike it rich. After the mountain men left, it wasn't long before miners arrived, looking for gold.

The first miners stood in ice-cold streams, swirling rocks and sand around in pans. Since gold is heavier than sand, it would settle at the bottom of the pan, making it easier to see.

If miners found "color," they might stake a claim. Staking a claim meant that they were the only ones who could take gold from that part of the stream.

The first major gold discovery, or strike, occurred in Montana in 1862 near what became the town of Bannack. When word got out that gold had been discovered, thousands of people rushed to Montana

to find their own pans full of gold. Other early strikes happened near Virginia City and Last Chance Gulch in Helena.

These mining camps all started off as rough and very rowdy places. But some of them grew into towns with stores, churches, and hotels. Most of the camps, however, were abandoned after miners stopped finding gold.

Today, what we call ghost towns are actually the last few buildings left over from some of these early gold or silver strikes.

Vigilantes

In the 1860s, Montana could be a lawless place. The new towns were filling up with young men, gold, and guns. There was almost no law enforcement.

As Bannack and Virginia City grew, outlaws, or "road agents," became a big problem. Miners would spend weeks building up their stake of gold only to see it stolen at gunpoint when they tried to sneak it out of the area.

A new sheriff, Henry Plummer, promised law and order. But when the crime wave only got worse after he was elected, some people thought that Plummer himself must be a road agent. They formed a "vigilance" group. These vigilantes began hanging people they thought were outlaws.

Plummer was one of their first victims.

The crime wave slowed down, but the cure may have been worse than the illness. The vigilantes hung enough people that no doubt there were some innocents among them.

These vigilantes were never held accountable for their deeds.

Henry Plummer

Indian Wars

In the West, most battles between Indian tribes and the Army were fought not long after the Civil War.

The United States wanted more people to come live in the West, but Indians were already here. This was their home.

The two sides tried to negotiate agreements called treaties. Most treaties said that the Indians would live in certain areas and be paid a certain amount of money for letting the US build roads and establish settlements. But many of the treaties were flawed by misunderstandings, and the US often didn't live up to its side of the agreements.

The Indians resented the broken treaties, and resisted being relocated to places that suited only the US. Armed conflicts often resulted.

In Montana, the Sioux, Cheyenne, Blackfeet, and Nez Perce were some of the fiercest fighters.

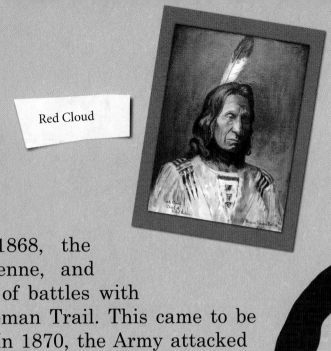

Red Cloud

Between 1866 and 1868, the Lakota, Northern Cheyenne, and Arapaho fought a series of battles with the Army along the Bozeman Trail. This came to be called Red Cloud's War. In 1870, the Army attacked a peaceful camp of Piegan Blackfeet on the Marias River, killing almost 200 people, mostly women, children, and old men. Today we call this the Marias Massacre.

The Crow tribe sometimes found it better to cooperate with the US. But the last battle between Indians in Montana and the US was fought by the Crow. That skirmish (or small battle) happened in 1887.

Battle at Little Bighorn

Sitting Bull

If there's one conflict that Montana is famous for, it's the battle on a small river called the Little Bighorn.

George Custer was a successful Civil War officer. He was flashy, handsome, and popular. Some people even thought that he should run for president. But he was also arrogant and reckless. When the Civil War ended, he was sent West to help fight Indians. In retrospect, it probably wasn't a perfect fit.

In 1876, he was ordered to find and confront a group of Sioux and Northern Cheyenne Indians, and then force them onto a reservation.

On June 25, 1876, Custer and his 7th Cavalry attacked a huge village. More than 1,500 warriors responded. They were led by a famous Sioux warrior named Sitting Bull. Three hours later, Custer and his men were dead.

This was an important battle. It was the last big victory for Indians in the West, and because Custer was so famous, it also made the rest of the US fear the Indians even more.

Custer

Flight of the Nez Perce

In 1877, about 700 Nez Perce Indians fled from their home in Eastern Oregon. They were trying to avoid being resettled. The Army wanted to force them onto a reservation in Northern Idaho.

Beginning in June, they fled through Western Montana and Yellowstone National Park, then north toward Canada. They fought and won several battles along the way.

Their final battle was on the Bear Paw Battlefield near what is now Chinook, Montana. After a journey of almost 1,200 miles, they were stopped just 40 miles from the Canadian border.

An encampment of 500 women and children, with fewer than 100 warriors, was attacked by 400 troops and 40 scouts led by General Nelson Miles. It was very cold, and the Nez Perce were freezing and starving.

Chief Joseph

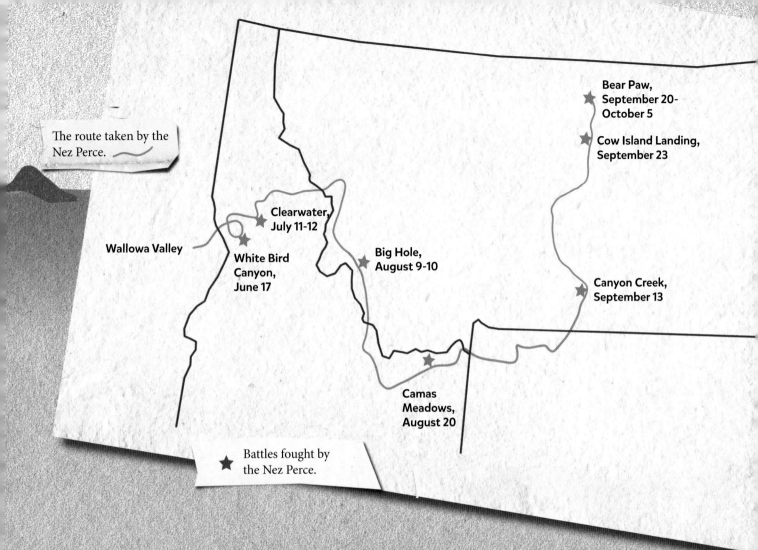

The route taken by the Nez Perce.

Bear Paw, September 20-October 5

Cow Island Landing, September 23

Clearwater, July 11-12

Wallowa Valley

White Bird Canyon, June 17

Big Hole, August 9-10

Canyon Creek, September 13

Camas Meadows, August 20

★ Battles fought by the Nez Perce.

After a long battle, the Nez Perce had no choice but to surrender.

Chief Joseph, one of the leaders, gave a famous speech in which he said, "I will fight no more forever."

Steamboats

It used to be very hard to get to Montana. Before railroads, one of the most important methods of travel was by steamboat up the Missouri River.

Steamboats were ships that used steam from boiling water to power large paddle wheels. Paddles churned the water and moved the ship forward. Traveling upstream, most of them moved only a little faster than a person could walk.

Steamboats needed a deep river to function, and so could only travel into Montana as far as Fort Benton.

Because it was the steamboat terminus, or end of the line, for a few years Fort Benton was one of the most important

White cliffs of the Missouri River

towns in the West. If you were eager to reach the gold fields of Montana, and if you could afford the $120 ticket, you went to Fort Benton on a steamboat.

There were also routes over dry land into Montana. These included the Mullan Road from Walla Walla, Washington, the Corinne Road from Corinne, Utah, the Bozeman Trail from Fort Laramie, Wyoming, and the Northern Overland Route, from the east. But these were slow and dangerous. In Montana's early years, steamboats were the most desirable way to travel.

Then the railroads came.

Butte, America

In the 1800s, Montana saw a lot of gold and silver strikes. Towns with names like Garnet, Castle Town, and Elkhorn all had their days in the sun. But as the strikes dried up, the towns did as well.

One of the most successful strikes occurred in Butte. The first Butte miners dug for gold. And then, just as the gold started to run out, they found silver. And while the silver was nice, they soon found something even more interesting: copper.

By the 1880s, America was starting to use electricity. But electricity needs wiring, and most wires are made out of copper. For the next hundred years or so, Butte helped electrify our country. Butte miners dug up so much copper that it would have been enough to pave a four-lane highway four inches deep, from Butte to Salt Lake City, Utah.

Mining is often very necessary, but it can also be harmful to the environment. After the biggest mines took what they could from Butte, they closed up shop. And after they closed, they left behind a bunch of problems that we're still trying to solve today.

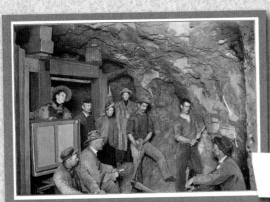

Butte's Parrot Mine, 1900

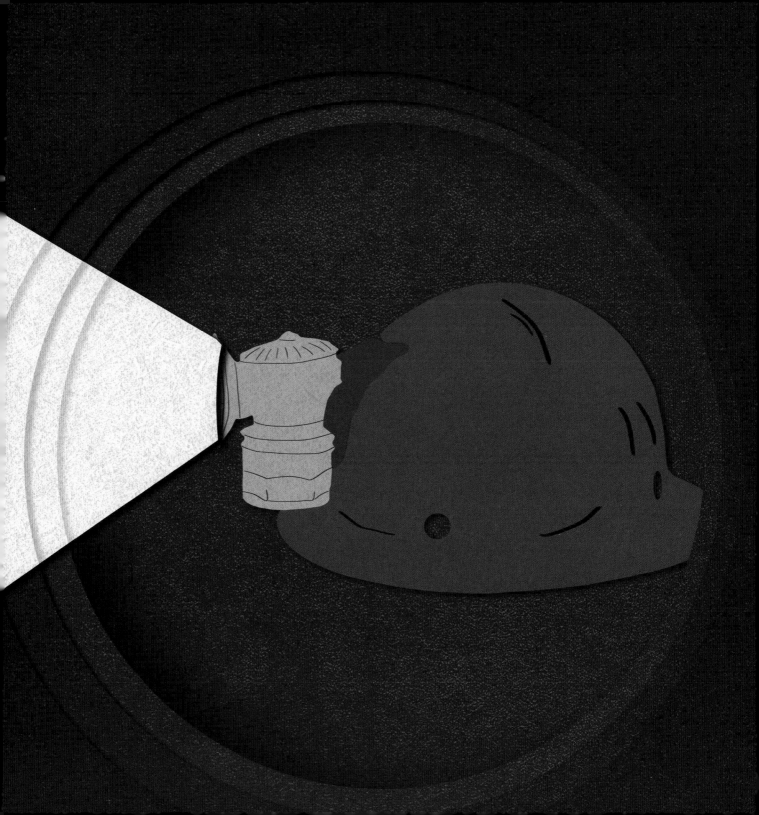

Copper Kings

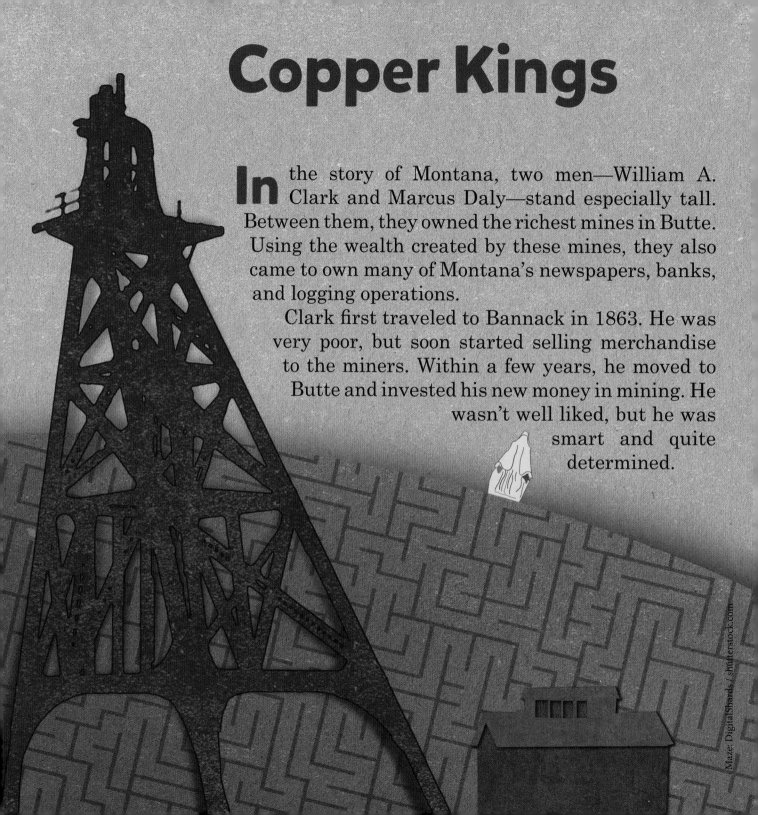

In the story of Montana, two men—William A. Clark and Marcus Daly—stand especially tall. Between them, they owned the richest mines in Butte. Using the wealth created by these mines, they also came to own many of Montana's newspapers, banks, and logging operations.

Clark first traveled to Bannack in 1863. He was very poor, but soon started selling merchandise to the miners. Within a few years, he moved to Butte and invested his new money in mining. He wasn't well liked, but he was smart and quite determined.

William A. Clark

Marcus Daly

F. Augustus Heinze

Marcus Daly was an Irish immigrant. He came to Butte in 1876 and also began investing in mines. He was either very lucky, very smart, or both, and it wasn't long before he controlled much of the city.

When Clark ran for political office in 1888, Daly helped defeat him. The two men became lifelong enemies. Their dislike for each other colored Montana's politics and economy for years. When Montanans had to vote on the location of the state capital, for instance, Daly wanted Anaconda but Clark wanted Helena. They spent around $1,500,000 promoting their favorite cities. When Clark later ran for the US Senate (bribing his way to victory) Daly worked against him.

A third copper king, F. Augustus Heinze, arrived later, and quickly became a rival.

But even as these men argued and fought, Butte prospered, and Montana prospered with it.

Railroads

As miners found strike after strike, people began to realize that there was a lot of money to be made in Montana. But the money was hard to get to, and it was also hard to get out.

By the early 1880s, railroads were being built in what was then Montana Territory. The first one was called the Utah and Northern Railroad. Two more railroads—the Great Northern and the Northern Pacific—arrived a few years later. The Chicago, Milwaukee, St. Paul and Pacific Railroad came in 1907.

Railroads in Montana changed everything. Miners and mining companies could now bring in heavy machinery and ship out their raw ore to be processed. Ranchers could more readily move their sheep and cattle, and homesteaders could travel to their new farms. It was also easier for tourists to visit Yellowstone National Park.

With railroads stitching their way across Montana, journeys that might have taken weeks, months, or even years could now be done in hours or days.

Montana met the world, and the world met Montana.

Influence of the Railroads

The railroads arrived in Montana just when the state was ready to really prosper. The railroads were so important, they came to hold a lot of influence in the state.

If one of the railroads decided to lay its tracks close to a certain town, that meant the town was likely to thrive. Sometimes railroads even helped establish new towns. The city of Billings was named for a railroad executive, and so were the towns of Dillon, Livingston, and Harlowton.

The US government liked the idea of building railroads, so they gave away pieces of land to help cover expenses. The railroads could use or sell the ground. By 1900, the Northern Pacific was the largest landowner in Montana.

James J. Hill was a railroad tycoon known for the Great Northern Railroad. He was called the "Empire Builder" for the way he opened up the Northwest. His route through Northern Montana became known as the Hi-line.

Logging

As the miners in Butte dug deeper underground, they used wooden beams to support their tunnels. A new ore smelter in Anaconda needed firewood in order to melt out the copper. And when railroads came to Montana, they needed timbers to hold up the tracks and trestles.

Somebody needed to supply all that wood.

By 1890, lumber mills were appearing all over Montana, cutting and sawing and shaping trees. The men who cut down the trees usually worked together in camps, and were called sawyers. After a sawyer cut down a tree, other men in the camp worked with axes to trim the limbs off. Then the downed trees were transported to the mills. The logs were often scooted off the mountain on greased chutes before being moved again on rail cars or floated down a river.

This was all dangerous, dirty, tiring work. And before we knew better, it was often very hard on the land as well. But all that wood went to good use, helping Montana grow.

Before chainsaws, sawyers used two-man crosscut saws, sometimes called "misery whips."

Homesteaders

From 1862, with a new law called the Homestead Act, the United States began giving away parcels of land to farmers. But in order for a "homesteader" to get a free parcel, he or she had to build a house, farm the ground, and live there for a certain period of time.

The first homesteaders in the Midwest were each given 160 acres of land. That wasn't enough to make a living on, though. Over time, the allotment increased. In some areas, a homesteader could finally receive up to 640 acres.

The railroads saw homesteading as a great way to sell tickets, and so they helped the government promote the idea. Between 1910 and 1922, homesteaders acquired more than 40 percent of Montana.

Homesteading was a lonely, hard life. And there were harder times to come. When they found that they couldn't make a living on 320 or often even 640 acres, most homesteaders ended up selling or abandoning their small farms. Today, many of the big ranches in Montana are made up of a number of these original homestead parcels.

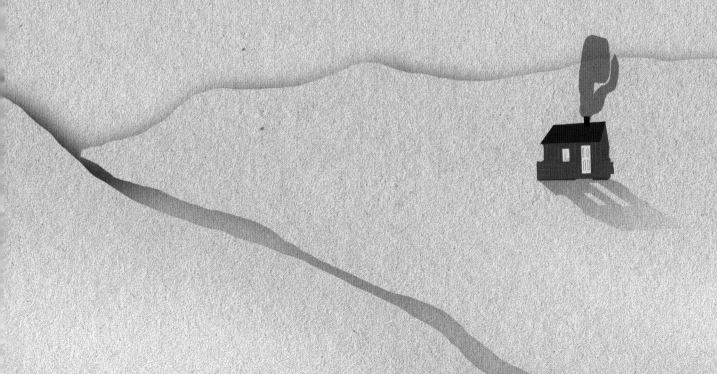

Ranching

There were a few cattle in Montana in the 1840s and 1850s, but there weren't a *lot* of cattle until the 1860s, when they were brought here to help feed miners.

In 1866, a miner named Nelson Story went to Texas and bought a herd of 600 longhorns. He and two dozen cowboys drove the herd 1,400 miles toward the Montana gold camps. After he succeeded, more Texas cattle drives soon followed.

In the 1870s and 1880s, the US stole back more of the land that had been ceded to the Indians. It was very unfair, but it made more of Montana available for open-range grazing. Open range meant that there were no fences.

Then came the winter of 1886 and 1887. For years, ranchers had been grazing too many cattle and not putting up enough hay to feed them in the winter. When this hard winter came, many of the cattle died, and a lot of the ranchers went out of business.

Ranchers soon began running fewer cattle and putting up more hay. They also started stringing wire (building fences) to keep their cattle in one place. The open-range era was over. You might say that modern Montana had begun.

Hidden History

The history of a place is always written from a point of view. No matter how hard a writer tries to be objective, he or she will always see the world in a certain way. For most of Montana's history, our stories were written by middle-aged white guys. (That's me, too: *I'm* a middle-aged white guy.) These writers would tend to write about other white guys.

But Montana and the West have been far more diverse and interesting than that.

For instance: Did you know that one out of every four or five cowboys in the late 1800s was African American? After the Civil War ended in 1865, these men went to Texas looking for work. Many of them ended up hiring on to the cattle drives.

And did you know that Chinese immigrants helped build many of the first roads, bridges, and railroad lines of the West? And they faced some of the worst discrimination in America's history while they did it.

And for every famous man who made the history books, there was almost always a woman beside him, working just as hard, who didn't see her story told at all.

When you consider everything that's been ignored, it's worth thinking about what kind of history is being written today. What stories are we telling now? And what stories are we forgetting?

Acknowledgments

Most of the information in this book came from other books about our state's history. I really like K. Ross Toole's *Montana: An Uncommon Land*, Joseph Kinsey Howard's *Montana: High, Wide, and Handsome*, and especially *Montana: Stories of the Land* by Krys Holmes.

Russell Rowland's book *Fifty-Six Counties: A Montana Journey* and Aaron Parrett's book *Montana: Then and Now* are both awesome, awesome reads.

Montana for Kids: The Story of Our State should just be the start of your journey. Happy reading!